*In memory of my parents' ancestry
and to my son, Hunter Danforth Paulsen.*

Copyright © 2025 Henry Paulsen

All rights reserved. No part of this publication may be reproduced, distributed, or transmitted in any form or by any means, including photocopying, recording, or other electronic or mechanical methods, without the prior written permission of the publisher, except in the case of brief quotations embodied in critical reviews and certain other noncommercial uses permitted by copyright law. For permission requests, write to the publisher, addressed" Attention: Permissions Coordinator," at the address below.

Paperback ISBN: 978-1-63616-258-4
eBook ISBN: 978-1-63616-260-7

Published By Opportune Independent Publishing Co.
Illustrations by Lena Pineda

Printed in the United States of America

For permission requests:
Email the publisher with the subject line as "Attention: Permissions Coordinator" to info@opportunepublishing.com

Table of Contents

CHAPTER 1: The Emergence of Skondarg	5
CHAPTER 2: The Ship Builder	9
CHAPTER 3: Skondarg and Crew	13
CHAPTER 4: Voyage to East Anglia	17
CHAPTER 5: Battle of Framlingham	21
CHAPTER 6: Homeward Bound to Denmark	27
CHAPTER 7: Roskilde and Journey to West Englia	31
CHAPTER 8: Lyflin and Onward to Cambria	35
CHAPTER 9: Skondarg and Heather—A Union Built	39
CHAPTER 10: Skondarg and His Legacy	43

CHAPTER 1
The Emergence of Skondarg

The story of Skondarg begins in 9th century Denmark. King Harold, The Bluetooth, rules over Denmark and Norway. King Harold is credited for being the first Viking ruler to Christianize Scandinavia. Many revered him, yet some opposed him due to their Norse mythological beliefs.

On the Island of Samso, which is east of the mainland, there was a 50-acre farm owned by a Christian Viking named Rasmus. The year was 970 AD. Rasmus and his wife, Anine, grew new potatoes, wheat, vegetables and had a flock of sheep. They were expecting their first child, and on June 7th of that year, their son was born. Rasmus named him Skondarg.

As a young boy, Skondarg learned much from his father. He was taught how to plant potatoes, wheat, vegetables and how to herd and fleece their sheep.

Since they were in close proximity to the ocean, Rasmus taught Skondarg how to fish, and when Skondarg became a teenager, he journeyed by boat with his father twice a year, hauling their harvested crops and woolen fleece across the straits to Odense and Aarhus to sell or trade for feed and supplies for their farm. Learning the techniques of his father on how to negotiate sales or trade proved to be an invaluable experience for him, which he employed throughout his life.

During his youth, Skondarg knew that he must become a skilled warrior to defend himself and his family in order to survive and succeed. He befriended Gunnar from the nearby village of Nordby. Gunnar had fought for King Harold in numerous battles through the years and was an excellent instructor for Skondarg. Through trial and error, Skondarg slowly but surely mastered the art of battle under Gunnar's guidance.

In 990 AD, when Skondarg turned 20 years old, suddenly a deadly virus hit the Island of Samso. Rasmus and Anine caught the virus and became feverish and weak.

Skondarg sought help from a lach in Nordby. Oluf had been a lach for over 20 years and came to treat Rasmus and Anine at their home.

Since they were sick and bedridden, Oluf applied various herbs to them and leeches to extract the virus. After several days of treatment, nothing was healing them, and they slowly became weaker and succumbed to their deaths.

Skondarg mourned the loss of his parents for days and buried them behind the farm. He reflected on his life, what to do next, and decided to sell the farm and become a ship builder. Skondarg yearned to become a good ship builder, sold his farm to his friend Gunnar and departed to Aarhus to start a new life.

CHAPTER 2

The Ship Builder

In the Spring of 994 AD, Skondarg arrives in Aarhus. Weary after his journey at sea, he rests on the shore. The next day, he seeks work with a local ship builder, and after looking at the craftsmanship of a few ship builders, he likes what one ship building crew is constructing and speaks to their crew leader, Ulrik. Skondarg convinces Ulrik that he has the skills to build Viking ships and would like to join his crew. Ulrik tells Skondarg that he just lost a worker and is willing to try him out. Skondarg quickly learns the craft of ship building. With 10 builders on his team, it required thousands of hours to finish building their Viking longship. Skondarg cut and placed the plank boards and was helpful in making the oars and mast.

During the time he was bulding the ship, Skondarg got to know members of his team as well. They shared stories with him about great Viking adventurers and their conquests.

Ragnar, the Norse Viking who conquered East Ambria (Eastern England) thanks to the aid of his sons in 865 AD, who avenged his death by the Anglo-Saxons. Oleg, the Finnish Viking who battled the Taturs (Turks) and became Prince of Kiev (Russian – Belarus – Ukraine Region) in 882 AD. The Norse Viking, Rollo, who conquered and reigned over Northern France (Normandy) in 911 AD.

It took over a year to finish building their ship, and they had a joyous celebration upon its completion. In building a beautiful Viking longship, Skondarg felt this was quite an accomplishment in his life, but he had higher aspirations. The Viking sagas he had heard inspired him to carry on his father Rasmus's legacy as a tradesman. Skondarg decided he wanted to journey to East Ambria and trade Danish goods with those people. In order to make that expedition, he set sail for Roskilde, the hub of land and sea trade founded by King Harold — The Bluetooth.

The Legend of Mighty Skondarg

CHAPTER 3

Skondarg and Crew

After facing rough, storm-like weather and nearly losing his boat at sea on his journey south, Skondarg finally arrives in Roskilde. To his good fortune, he runs into Olaf, Gunnar's farmhand, in Samso. Olaf tells Skondarg that he recently arrived with new potatoes, fleece and leather and that he too is seeking to join a Viking trade expedition to East Anglia. They talk to several tradesmen around the Roskilde Bay and come upon a tough, warrior-like Danish Viking named Ivar.

Ivar told them that he was in the middle of recruiting crews for two longships to set sail for East Anglia soon, and that they were welcome to join if they would assist him in completing recruitment of the right men for this expedition.

Ivar knew that he had to have crews that were battle-tested in order for trade with the Anglo-Saxons to be successful and insisted that Skondarg and Olaf be very selective.

They scoured Roskilde and neighboring villages, approaching numerous able-bodied Vikings, and after three long, laborious weeks, hand-picked and recruited 25 new crew members to finish completing the crews of 35 for each ship.

The crews loaded their ships with various goods, including potatoes, spices, wool, leather, iron, and silver. They stocked food supplies and prepared the longships for departure. Ivar captained the lead ship, while a Norse Viking named Hans commanded the second.

It was now Fall of 996 AD, and the two Viking longships pulled out of Roskilde and set sail for East Anglia, not knowing what they may encounter on this journey but courageously prepared nonetheless.

The Legend of Mighty Skondarg

CHAPTER 4

Voyage to East Anglia

Ivar, who captained the lead Viking longship with his crew of men including Skondarg and Hans, set sail heading north up the Kattegat Sea between Eastern Denmark and Western Sweden. All went well, and in a day's time, they rounded the northern tip of Denmark and began to sail southwest on the Skagettak Sea as they journeyed en route to the North Sea and Engla Land (England).

Day two of their voyage went smoothly, sailing on the Skagettak until they hit turbulent waters entering the open North Sea. A storm front approached Ivar's and Hans's boats as they rocked up and down in choppy waters, high winds and heavy rainfall for over two hours.

Fortunately, they braved the storm and continued south down the North Sea to East Anglia on the southeast coast of Engla Land.

All went well over the next three days on their journey sailing southward to East Anglia. On the morning of the sixth day, they entered the large bay of East Anglia and landed on the shore. The men were weary and set up encampment, fished for food, ate and rested. The following day, Ivar and crew climbed up a cliff to the mainland. Hans and crew stayed on the shore to guard the longships with their goods and supplies.

The Legend of Mighty Skondarg

CHAPTER 5

Battle of Framlingham

Ivar, Skondarg and their men were now on the mainland of Mercia (Ancient Southeast England) and journeyed by foot for a few miles to the Village of Framlingham. As they entered Framlingham, some of the villagers stepped out in front of them, and Skondarg shouted, "We are Christian Vikings who come in peace to sell or trade our goods with you!" The villagers accepted this and invited Ivar and crew to meet at their Framlingham Inn to discuss this further.

They all sat down at the Inn. Ivar shared what goods they brought to sell or trade with the villagers, and the villagers told him what goods they were currently short on or completely out of. They all came to a mutual agreement in which Ivar and Hans's crew of men would return the next day with all goods requested at the Framlingham Market Square.

It was now Thursday, a day of the week derived from the Vikings as Thor's Day. By mid-morning, Ivar and Hans arrived in the market square with the villagers present and ready to look over and negotiate on all the goods they wanted to purchase or trade with them. The Vikings brought an abundance of potatoes, spices, wool, leather, iron and silver. The villagers brought hone, salt, fish, wine and flax. Much was traded, with mainly iron and silver sold to the villagers.

One of the villagers who Skondarg met and traded with was a farmer named Danforth from nearby. Danforth tells Skondarg that he is being threatened by Barton of Mercia, who is a swindler and land thief. He asks Skondarg if he will help fend off this evil intruder and his men. Danforth also mentions that Barton has already seized a stream on his land that flows down to the bay and is already shipping supplies on it. Skondarg assures Danforth that he and his crew will immediately help defend Danforth and his land. Skondarg explains to Ivar what he and his men must do. They gather their men and follow Danforth to his stream to confront Barton. Skondarg and Ivar, along with eight others and Danforth, approach the stream and see Barton with seven of his men loading supplies onto three rafts.

Skondarg yells to them, demanding they permanently leave the area right now or they will be forced off Danforth's land. Barton replies that this stream is theirs and they will not leave. The Vikings led by Skondarg swiftly march with swords held high up to Barton and his men and begin to attack. The Battle of Framlingham has begun!

Barton and his men grab their swords and begin to fight. Skondarg steps in front of Barton and attacks him. While they duel, all men on both sides brutally attack each other. Within minutes, all seven of Barton's men had been stabbed to death, lying bloodied on the ground.

The Vikings suffered minor wounds, yet Ivar's youngest crewman, Armund, was severely wounded, lying dead as well. Skondarg and Barton continued dueling. Skondarg got slashed across his upper right arm, but he then slashed Barton's left leg and began to hobble. Skondarg forced Barton to slowly step back, then Barton suddenly tripped and fell backward over a rock and fell into the stream. Skondarg leaped into the stream and stabbed Barton right through the heart. As Barton lay dying there in the water, Skondarg said, "You, Barton, are no longer a menace to Mercia!"

After the battle, Danforth, who watched from nearby, walked up to Skondarg and thanked him for his valor, then took him and a couple of his men back to his cottage to tend to their injuries.

Susan, Danforth's wife, had Skondarg and his two Vikings sit down and tended to their wounds with water, wine and oil. She then dressed the wounds with cloth strips. Susan whipped up some porridge to feed them all. Danforth expressed his gratitude to Skondarg for fighting and defending his stream and land. Skondarg and his two men said it was a just and rightful honor to do so, then stood up, shook hands with Danforth and Susan and departed to Framlingham to pick up their remaining traded goods before heading back to the longships in the bay to rest for the night.

The Legend of Mighty Skondarg

CHAPTER 6
Homeward Bound to Denmark

It was morning on the bay beach. Ivar's and Hans's crews gathered up their belongings and loaded everything onto the longships and set sail, departing from Mercia. The two Viking vessels headed north up the North Sea, along the Engla Land coast. All was going well as they progressed up the coastline. By the time they reached Northeast Engla Land, from behind a cliff two large boats suddenly appeared, cut off the Viking ships and sidled up next to them.

A tall man wearing dark clothing shouted to Ivar and Hans that they have trespassed into Northeast Anglia Waters and must relinquish all that is on board. Ivar shouted back no and that they will leave the area, but before Ivar and Hans could shift their longships away, the men aboard the two invasive boats jumped onto the Viking ships and attacked Ivar's and Hans's crews.

The man wearing black and the leader of this marauding pack was Tyne. The people in this region called him Tyne the Terrible. Tyne and his 13 men quickly assaulted, making it difficult for the Vikings to defend themselves. Within minutes, two of Hans's men were stabbed and thrown overboard, yet Ivar, Skondarg and crew courageously fought off, killed and pushed eight of Tyne's men into the sea. Soon, there were only two marauders left battling, Tyne and his grim, bearded shipman, Alfred. Ivar knocked down Alfred and stabbed him in the chest with his sword. Skondarg then snuck behind Tyne and slit his throat. Tyne and Alfred too were thrown into the bloodied waters. Ivar and Skondarg rejoiced in victory but, to their misfortune, quickly noticed that over a third of their goods were gone.

The Vikings headed east and directly north up the North Sea. By the third day, they reached the Skagettak Sea and knew they were almost home. On the fourth day, the longships entered Danish waters. Both crews were weary and hungry due to lack of food. As the ships docked on the shore of Roskilde Bay, the men stepped onto the land, collapsed from exhaustion and rested there. Three of the crewmen went into town and got fish, bread and fruit for all. Their journey was now complete as they pondered what lay ahead.

CHAPTER 7

Roskilde and Journey to West Englia

Skondarg and six men from their crews decided to live in Roskilde, building or repairing longships. Skondarg noticed that Ulrik was still in charge of building some longships there, approached him and was re-hired. Now that Skondarg had a job, he quickly found a small cottage to live in near Roskilde. For the next year, he helped Ulrik and his team build two longships and did minor repairs for the owners of longships in the bay.

One day, Skondarg was working on repairing the hull of a longship with Varg. Varg told Skondarg about his 990 AD voyage to Eire, which is Ireland, and his visit to Dyflin, which became Dublin. Dyflin was a Norse Viking colony that was discovered in 873 AD. Varg shared his story on how much he enjoyed the time he spent with fellow Norsemen and heard about a land south of Eire called Cambria, which became Wales, which was a successful trading of goods experience.

Skondarg was inspired in hearing this and decided that he wanted to coordinate and lead a trade voyage to the western coast of Englia.

The next day, he talked to some of his fellow boat builders to see if they'd like to sell and trade goods in Cambria. Skondarg and Varg got 14 Vikings committed to going on this adventure. After the men had finished building another longship, they took a couple weeks off to gather potatoes, spices, wool, leather, iron and silver. Skondarg sailed up to Samso to visit Gunnar on the farm and paid him for several sacks of new potatoes. Gunnar was about to retire from farming. They talked about the past, and Skondarg wished him well as he departed south back to Roskilde.

It was May of 998 A.D. Skondarg's and Varg's crews began loading up their goods onto their longships. Varg brought two of his Swedish Valhunds with them and set sail for Dyflin. All went well until a storm forced them to land their ships on the shore of Dunnet Head at the northern tip of Scotland.

A few hours later, they sailed out and began to head south down the Eire Sea on their way to Dyflin. After five days at sea, they reached Dyflin Bay.

The Legend of Mighty Skondarg

CHAPTER 8

Lyflin and Onward to Cambria

Skondarg's and Varg's crews entered Dyflin and went to Liffey Ordbog Inn, where many went to eat, drink and rest. The men enjoyed food and ale, then slept at Liffey's for a few nights. They sold some of their goods to the local Vikings and prepared to sail onward to Cambria.

All went well heading southeast down the Eire Sea until a dark, mysterious ship appeared. Skondarg and Varg were concerned that they may be attacked by what may have been an Englia ship, but fortunately, the large ship continued north as it passed by their longships.

By midday on their second day at sea, they rounded the southwestern tip of Cambria and soon reached Pembrokeshire Bay.

When they docked, Skondarg noticed a young woman and older man fishing from a dock. He yelled that they came in peace to trade and sell goods. Both crews stepped onto the docks and were led into town to the Pembrokeshire Inn. Even though in years past, Vikings had attacked Pembrokeshire, the people reservedly welcomed Skondarg and Varg.

That afternoon, the Vikings traded and sold most of their supplies to the local people and celebrated with them. The young woman, Heather, and her father, Arwyn, sat down with Skondarg and Varg. They talked about their lives growing up as farmers in Scandinavia and Cambria. Heather and Skondarg took a liking to one another and spent the rest of the evening getting to know each other.

The next morning, Skondarg and Varg met and decided they wanted to stay in Pembrokeshire for a while. They asked their crews who wanted to stay, and several of them agreed it was a nice place to live as well. At noon, Arwyn dropped by. Skondarg and Varg asked him if he knew of any open land where they could farm. Arwyn told them that there were a couple hundred acres available four miles north of town and showed them the land later that afternoon. Skondarg and Varg liked what they saw and began making plans to build their farms.

The Legend of Mighty Skondarg

CHAPTER 9
Skondarg and Heather—A Union Built

As Skondarg and Heather's relationship grew, he and Varg gathered the wood supplies needed from the area to begin building their new homes. They got a few of their Viking crewmen who stayed in Pembrokeshire to help in the construction. It took them several months to finish building their homes, which were similar in design. Once their homes were built, Skondarg , Varg and friends celebrated at the Pembrokeshire Inn. Heather and her father joined in the celebration.

That evening, Skondarg met privately with Heather, expressed his love for her and proposed marriage to her. She said yes. They kissed and hugged each other and set a date for their wedding at Pembrokeshire Church.

It was June 15th, 1001 AD, Skondarg and Heather's wedding day. They dressed appropriately for this special occasion. Varg was Skondarg's best man, and Laurie was Heather's maid of honor. 300 Pembrokeshire villagers attended the wedding service at Pembrokeshire Church. The Minister performed the proceeding, and the couple vowed their love for each other forever. All rejoiced, and afterward, Skondarg and Heather moved into their new home.

After they settled in, Skondarg gathered rye, wheat, oats, peas and new potato seeds from the area and began planting their crops. He also helped Varg plant his crops on his land. Varg, with his two Swedish Valhunds, and Skondarg sought to breed the dogs with a dog owner in Pembrokeshire. Laurie, Heather's friend, knew a man who had Pomeranians he wanted to breed. They met with Aidan and bred Varg's male Valhunds with two of Aidan's female Pomeranians.

Within three months, the Pomeranians had litters of 10 and eight puppies. A new herding dog breed was born, the Pembroke Welsh Corgi. It was a great moment for them, and by fall, the young pups were brought back to Skondarg's and Varg's farms.

The Legend of Mighty Skondarg

CHAPTER 10

Skondarg and His Legacy

In Winter of 1001 AD, Heather shared exciting news with Skondarg. She was pregnant with their first child, and on August 27th of 1002 AD, a baby boy was born. They named him Magnus, which means "Great." Varg and friends celebrated this joyous occasion with Skondarg and Heather. Skondarg and Varg fenced in their land, and through trade, which included giving up six of their Corgis, they we able to gather livestock. They got several sheep, pigs, goats and a few horses for their farms. The Corgis on both farms were well trained by their masters to herd the livestock into their pens and down the country road to Pembrokeshire to be slaughtered.

Another momentous day took place for Skondarg and Heather on October 2nd of 1004 AD.

Their second child, a baby girl, was born. They named her Megan, which means "Pearl." When Magnus and Megan were old enough, they began to help with chores on the farm. Magnus assisted Skondarg with the crops and livestock, while Megan assisted Heather with cooking and keeping up the household. As a family, they went into town to visit with their friends and fish off the Pembrokeshire Bay. Overall, the years were good to them. Magnus, now 21 years old, and Megan, who just turned 18, continued to work on the farm. Whenever Varg was short-handed, Magnus would help him finish chores on his farm as well.

One day in the early Spring of 2022 AD, Skondarg was planting new potato seeds when he suddenly felt a harsh, sudden pain in his chest and collapsed onto the ground. He instantly died of a severe heart attack. A Corgi named Darby, which means "Keeper of the Estate," noticed that something was wrong and barked repeatedly until Magnus, who was working on the other side of the farm, came running to see what was wrong. Magnus quickly realized that his father had died. He went over to get Varg to help carry Skondarg's remains back to the farmhouse. The family mourned the loss of Skondarg. Later that day, they covered up Skondarg and carted him into Pembrokeshire.

Magnus and Megan gathered their Viking friends at the Pembrokeshire Inn and decided that it was best to honor Skondarg by providing a traditional Viking funeral. They placed Skondarg's body in his longship, gathered small branches and twigs from nearby and placed them on top and around his body. His family placed a few personal items of his in the ship as well.

Others from the town gathered on the docks and Magnus led them in prayer, in which they wished Skondarg true happiness in the afterlife. Varg and a fellow Viking lit their torches, then lit the branches on fire. They shoved the ship out into the bay, ablaze. After the ship burned up, Skondarg's remains cremated and sunken into the bay, Heather, Magnus, Megan and friends went to the Pembrokeshire Inn to feast and reflect on Skondarg's life accomplishments. Several at the feast were in agreement that Skondarg was a truly courageous and adventurous hero who should always be recognized with the likes of Erik the Red and his son, Leif Erikson.

www.ingramcontent.com/pod-product-compliance
Lightning Source LLC
Chambersburg PA
CBHW061742070526
44585CB00024B/2777